RO

THE
TEMPLE OF
THE SUN

BY

EMMA THOMAS

THE
TEMPLE OF
THE SUN

KENSINGTON & CHELSEA LIBRARIES SERVICE	
513035	
000633	
PETERS	J985.019
M 08 OCT 2005	

ticktock
MEDIA

Copyright © ticktock Entertainment Ltd 2003
First published in Great Britain in 2003 by ticktock Media Ltd.,
Unit 2, Orchard Business Centre, North Farm Road, Tunbridge Wells, Kent, TN2 3XF
We would like to thank: Nick Owen, Dr. Colin McEwan at The British Museum, Elizabeth Wiggans
and the people of the Patacancha Valley, Peru.
ISBN 1 86007 374 3 PB
ISBN 1 86007 380 8 HB
Printed in Egypt
A CIP catalogue record for this book is available from the British Library.

All rights reserved. No part of this publication may be reproduced, copied, stored in a retrieval system,
or transmitted in any form or by any means electronic, mechanical, photocopying, recording or otherwise
without prior written permission of the copyright owner.

Would you like to join an exciting expedition to Peru?

The experts featured in the story, Dr. McLeish and Dr. Orellana, are fictional. But real facts about historians and archaeologists have been used to give you an accurate picture of the work they do. Sam Owen, Padre Luis, Mr. Mallender and the Barking family are also fictional; as are the highland village of Yanacocha and the mummy that is discovered there. But the characteristics of the mummy, details about the lives of the Incas and information about life in the highlands of Peru today are all based on fact.

Interested to know more? Ready to go exploring?

Then welcome to the City Museum...

CONTENTS

CITY MUSEUM PASS

Name: Dr. Elizabeth McLeish
Department: Head of Ancient Americas Department

Interests: History, exploring and hiking.

CITY MUSEUM PASS

Name: Sam Owen
Department: Ancient Americas — temporary research assistant

Interests: History, computers and football.

TEMPORARY

3

INCA TREASURES

Day 1

I've always loved the City Museum with its huge collection of exciting items from around the world. And now, here I am for the holidays helping Dr. Liz McLeish the curator, or head, of the 'Ancient Americas' department. Most of the artefacts in the gallery were left to the museum by Sir Cedric Barking, a Victorian explorer. When someone leaves an item to a museum in their will it is called a bequest. This is an important way for museums to obtain and safeguard rare and valuable items. Sir Cedric visited Peru in South America many times to study the history of the Inca people. Dr. McLeish has travelled to Peru as well. She did the fieldwork for her PhD in the mountains there.

This afternoon we had a meeting with Sir Cedric's grandson, Sir Dennis Barking. Some further artefacts have just been found in the family archive: a wooden goblet, a mysterious old letter and a fragment of woven cloth. Dr. McLeish is very excited. She is certain that the items are Inca!

Cuzco, Peru 18th August, 1887

Dear Sir Cedric,

Do you remember me telling you about the people of Yanacocha in the highlands? I enclose a fragment from a wonderful textile that comes from there. I have never seen anything like it; it seems to me to be ancient. I am sending the textile to you along with a wooden cup, and would value your expert opinion as to what they are.

By the way, Mr. Mallender has been helping me with my English. He says I am doing very well. What do you think?

Tu gran amigo,

Padre Luis

Summer 1999
Dr. McLeish's good friends in the mountains of Peru with one of their alpacas.

The textile design is similar to this very famous Inca artefact: the 'Dumbarton Oaks' tunic. The tunic is made from one piece of cloth sewn up the sides with openings for the arms and head.

These goblets were used for drinking beer in special rituals or celebrations. They are called 'keros' in Quechua, the language of the Incas. Quechua is still spoken in Peru today.

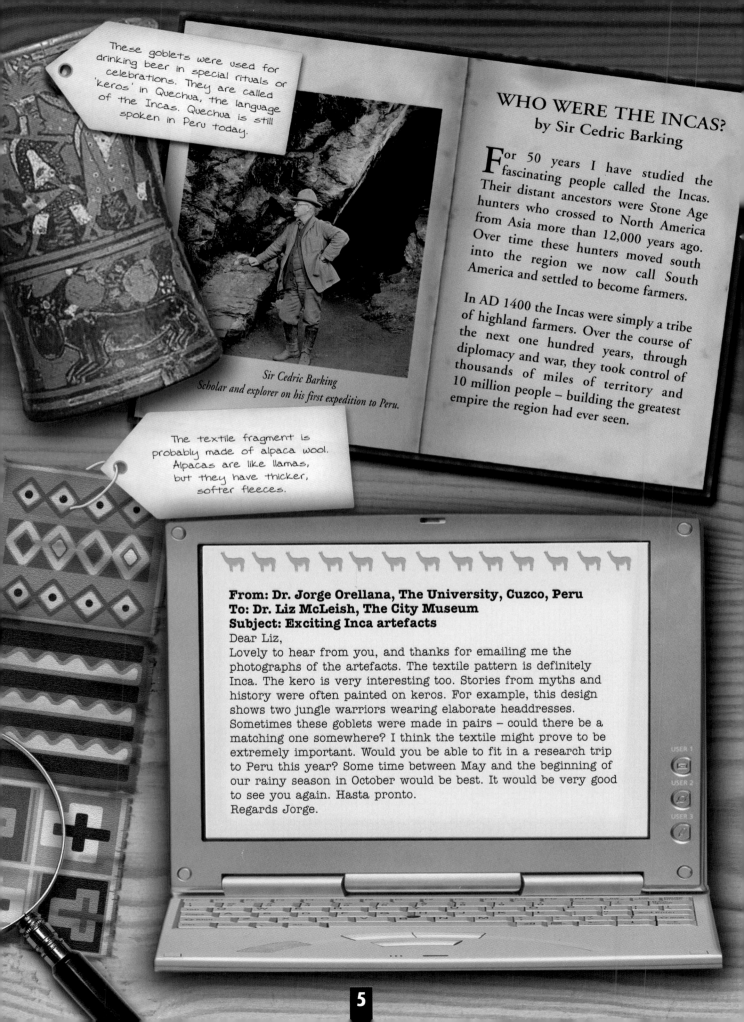

Sir Cedric Barking
Scholar and explorer on his first expedition to Peru.

The textile fragment is probably made of alpaca wool. Alpacas are like llamas, but they have thicker, softer fleeces.

WHO WERE THE INCAS?
by Sir Cedric Barking

For 50 years I have studied the fascinating people called the Incas. Their distant ancestors were Stone Age hunters who crossed to North America from Asia more than 12,000 years ago. Over time these hunters moved south into the region we now call South America and settled to become farmers.

In AD 1400 the Incas were simply a tribe of highland farmers. Over the course of the next one hundred years, through diplomacy and war, they took control of thousands of miles of territory and 10 million people – building the greatest empire the region had ever seen.

From: Dr. Jorge Orellana, The University, Cuzco, Peru
To: Dr. Liz McLeish, The City Museum
Subject: Exciting Inca artefacts

Dear Liz,
Lovely to hear from you, and thanks for emailing me the photographs of the artefacts. The textile pattern is definitely Inca. The kero is very interesting too. Stories from myths and history were often painted on keros. For example, this design shows two jungle warriors wearing elaborate headdresses. Sometimes these goblets were made in pairs – could there be a matching one somewhere? I think the textile might prove to be extremely important. Would you be able to fit in a research trip to Peru this year? Some time between May and the beginning of our rainy season in October would be best. It would be very good to see you again. Hasta pronto.
Regards Jorge.

A TRIP TO PERU

Day 10

I could hardly believe it when Dr. McLeish said that I could accompany her on a research trip to Peru. The Barking family have offered to pay for the expedition; so we are on our way!

Dr. McLeish tells me that South America is vast; Peru alone is the size of France, Spain and the UK put together. The territory that the Incas controlled extended beyond just Peru, stretching over 4,800 km from north to south. Their empire was rich in gold and silver too. Even today tin, copper, emeralds, silver and gold are mined in the region. Before the Incas there were other civilizations living along the Pacific coast. The rich resources of sea, shoreline and fertile river valleys made it an ideal place to settle.

We are flying south from Lima, the modern-day capital of Peru, into the Andes, the mountain chain that runs the length of South America. Our destination is Cuzco, the capital of the Incas.

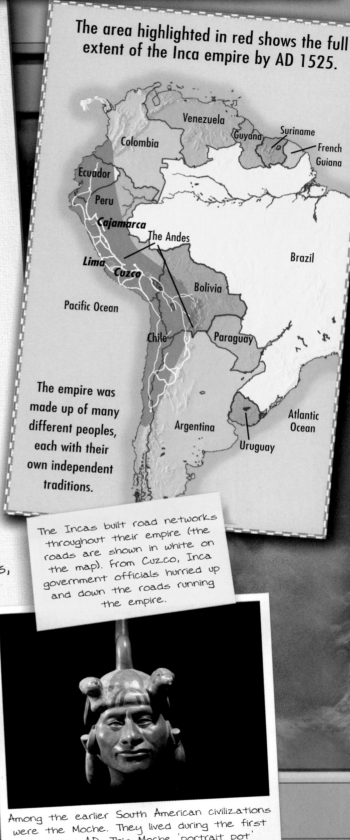

The area highlighted in red shows the full extent of the Inca empire by AD 1525.

The empire was made up of many different peoples, each with their own independent traditions.

The Incas built road networks throughout their empire (the roads are shown in white on the map). From Cuzco, Inca government officials hurried up and down the roads running the empire.

Among the earlier South American civilizations were the Moche. They lived during the first centuries AD. This Moche 'portrait pot' probably depicts one of their rulers.

Dr. McLeish has given me this fascinating book all about the destruction of the Inca empire. She says it's important for me to understand what happened to the Incas if I am going to help with historical research in Peru.

The Andes is the longest mountain range in the world.

THE STORY OF THE CONQUISTADORS

In 1532, a Spanish adventurer Francisco Pizarro and his band of 168 'Conquistadors' landed on the north coast of Peru. They had come from Spain in search of riches. When they arrived a civil war was raging between two branches of the Inca royal family.

One side was led by the Inca ruler Atahualpa. He agreed to meet for negotiations with Pizarro and his men, at the Inca town of Cajamarca. But the Spaniards tricked Atahualpa, taking him hostage. Atahualpa's followers collected an enormous ransom of gold and silver, but the Spaniards just took the treasure then ruthlessly murdered the Inca leader.

Francisco Pizarro on horseback. The Incas had no horses so the Spaniards had one great advantage in their conquest of Peru.

The Nazca people lived on the western desert coast in the first centuries AD. They created the 'Nazca Lines', mysterious drawings on the landscape.

Day 11

The city of Cuzco is very high up, over 3,400 metres above sea level. The altitude made me feel dizzy and a little sick at first. It is best to lie down for a few hours, but Dr. McLeish was so keen to see her old friend that we went straight to Dr. Orellana's office. To help us acclimatize he made us some coca leaf tea.

Dr. Orellana believes the piece of textile has been cut from a larger garment; almost certainly a male tunic, and possibly one that was made for a member of the Inca royal family. The small stains and encrustations on the fabric make him think that the tunic might even have been used to wrap an Inca mummy! I asked Dr. Orellana if it was possible the mummy could have survived. Dr. McLeish said that would be wonderful, but as the textile originally came from the highlands, where the climate is very damp, it would seem unlikely. Dr. Orellana smiled and handed us an interesting magazine clipping. He thinks it could be possible.

Cuzco University where
Dr. Orellana has his office.

A 17th century illustration by Guaman Poma de Ayala, who was half Inca and half Spanish. He wrote a fascinating illustrated history of the Incas. Historians can use his work in their research. This illustration confirms that Inca kings wore tunics decorated like our piece of weaving.

The designs in the boxes are known as 'tocapus'. Each tocapu probably had a particular significance, but historians have been unable to decipher them.

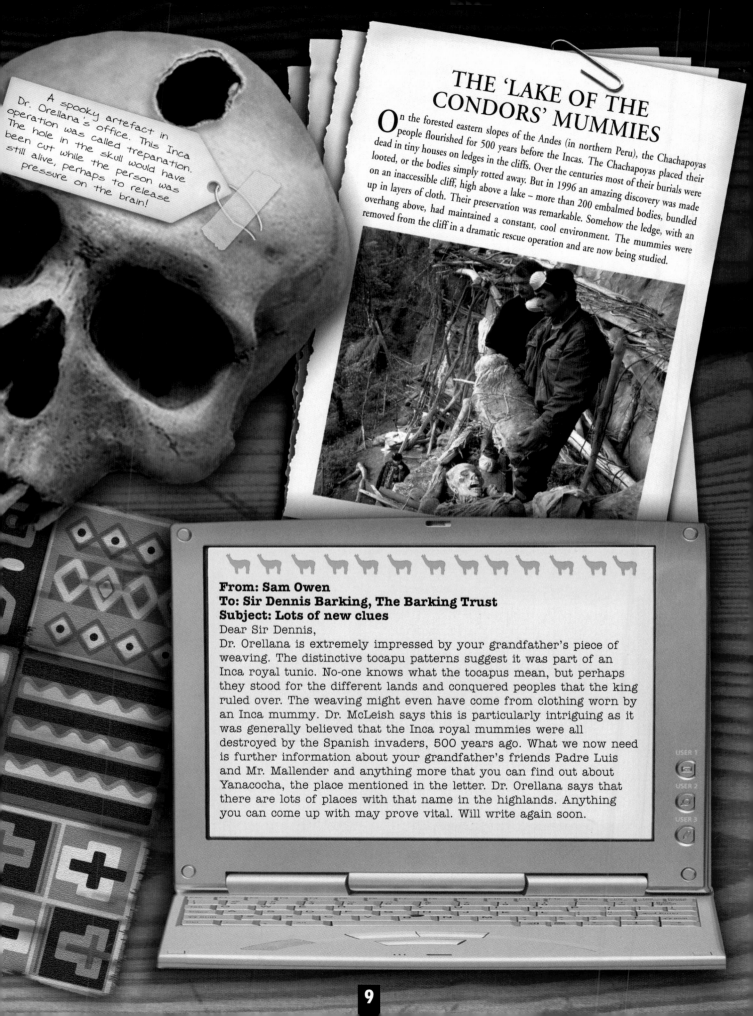

A spooky artefact in Dr. Orellana's office. This Inca operation was called trepanation. The hole in the skull would have been cut while the person was still alive, perhaps to release pressure on the brain!

THE 'LAKE OF THE CONDORS' MUMMIES

On the forested eastern slopes of the Andes (in northern Peru), the Chachapoyas people flourished for 500 years before the Incas. The Chachapoyas placed their dead in tiny houses on ledges in the cliffs. Over the centuries most of their burials were looted, or the bodies simply rotted away. But in 1996 an amazing discovery was made on an inaccessible cliff, high above a lake – more than 200 embalmed bodies, bundled up in layers of cloth. Their preservation was remarkable. Somehow the ledge, with an overhang above, had maintained a constant, cool environment. The mummies were removed from the cliff in a dramatic rescue operation and are now being studied.

From: Sam Owen
To: Sir Dennis Barking, The Barking Trust
Subject: Lots of new clues

Dear Sir Dennis,

Dr. Orellana is extremely impressed by your grandfather's piece of weaving. The distinctive tocapu patterns suggest it was part of an Inca royal tunic. No-one knows what the tocapus mean, but perhaps they stood for the different lands and conquered peoples that the king ruled over. The weaving might even have come from clothing worn by an Inca mummy. Dr. McLeish says this is particularly intriguing as it was generally believed that the Inca royal mummies were all destroyed by the Spanish invaders, 500 years ago. What we now need is further information about your grandfather's friends Padre Luis and Mr. Mallender and anything more that you can find out about Yanacocha, the place mentioned in the letter. Dr. Orellana says that there are lots of places with that name in the highlands. Anything you can come up with may prove vital. Will write again soon.

USER 1

USER 2

USER 3

THE INCA CAPITAL

Day 12

After an early night, I woke up full of energy. The air still feels thin though, and walking uphill is a struggle! The two doctors had lots of catching up to do, so today was a great opportunity for me to take a walk around Cuzco, the holy centre, or 'navel', of the Inca world.

In Inca times the main square was surrounded on every side by the palaces of the Inca rulers. Dr. McLeish says that when an Inca king died the palace he had occupied in life became a sacred place. The deceased ruler was not mummified and consigned to a tomb, as they did in ancient Egypt. He was embalmed and then kept in his palace. His closest relatives looked after him as if he were still alive, worshipping him as a god-like ancestor. Royal mummies were fed, clothed and regularly taken out to be paraded around the city. They even took part in important ceremonies.

Inca stonework is everywhere in Cuzco. Many of the walls of the Inca palaces still survive, supporting modern buildings.

Hi Mum and Dad,

This afternoon we visited Sacsahuaman, a sacred Inca site and fortress on the outskirts of Cuzco. It is a fantastic example of Inca stonemasonry. I 'm becoming quite expert on the Incas and South American mummies. This postcard shows a mummy from the Peruvian coast; it is about 2,000 years old and was marvellously preserved by the dry desert conditions. I'm really hoping that I get to see an actual Inca mummy before we leave!

An Inca royal mummy is carried aloft in a procession.

The ramparts of the fortress of Sacsahuaman were made from massive blocks, each weighing up to 100 tonnes. They fitted together so perfectly that no mortar was used.

It is said that Sacsahuaman took 30,000 men up to 30 years to build.

THE STORY OF THE CONQUISTADORS

After Atahualpa's murder, his enemies became Pizarro's allies. The Spanish Conquistadors marched on Cuzco, and a young prince called Manco was made king, with Spanish support, in December 1533. But Pizarro and his Conquistadors betrayed Manco too. They ransacked the empire and took control. The Inca people were abused and their treasures plundered.

More and more invaders were coming from Spain. Realising that the Inca empire was on the brink of destruction, Manco secretly fled Cuzco, gathered his forces and laid siege to the city. Manco's army almost succeeded in destroying the Spaniards, but Spanish reinforcements arrived just in time.

The Conquistadors even stripped and melted down the gold and silver that decorated the holiest Inca temple – the Temple of the Sun, in Cuzco.

This gold and silver maize cob is from the temple's artificial garden. All the plants in the garden were made from precious metals.

The curved wall of the original Temple of the Sun can be seen today incorporated into the church of Santo Domingo.

Cuzco City Plan

Cuzco was built under the direction of the greatest of all the Inca rulers, Pachacuti. Some said that the city was laid out in the shape of a puma, a sacred animal to the Incas.

Sacsahuaman

The central square

The temple of the sun

Day 15

What an incredible trip this is turning out to be. I felt sure that I was going to spend hours digging up old ruins, but studying history in Peru isn't like that at all. The history of the Incas is all around us! Dr. McLeish and I have moved on to the Inca town of Ollantaytambo. It was built on the Urubamba river, in an area that is known as the 'Sacred Valley of the Incas'. Dr. McLeish worked here for many years, and helped the community to set up a small museum. The museum has displays on the history of Ollantaytambo, and it highlights many of the Inca traditions that are still maintained by the local people today.

From the town you can see giant steps going up the mountainside. Dr. McLeish tells me that these 'agricultural terraces', with their stone retaining walls, were built by the Incas. They protect against soil erosion, providing enough good, flat land for growing food. The main crop grown in the valley was, and still is, maize: the sacred crop of the Incas.

Dr. McLeish had some chicha (maize beer) with her old friends from Ollantaytambo. I tried a sip too! In the old days we would have drunk from wooden keros.

Maize cobs drying in the sun. Some will be sold and the rest kept for cooking or making beer.

Maize was a versatile crop. It could be boiled, toasted, eaten on the cob or ground to make flour.

THE STORY OF THE CONQUISTADORS

When the siege of Cuzco failed, Manco and his army retreated and occupied the town of Ollantaytambo. They strengthened the town with extra walls and fortifications and even managed to resist a Spanish attack, inflicting a rare defeat on the Spanish invaders. But Manco knew that he was vulnerable in Ollantaytambo. He had to retreat to a place where the Spaniards couldn't find him.

So, according to Inca history, in 1537 Manco left Ollantaytambo for Vilcabamba, a remote region of mountains and jungle. He was accompanied, it is said, by his wives, sons, vast herds of llamas and alpacas, thousands of his followers and the mummies of his royal ancestors.

Some of the residents of Ollantaytambo. They are wearing a mixture of traditional and modern clothes.

From: Dr. Jorge Orellana, The University, Cuzco, Peru
To: Sam Owen
Subject: Pachacuti – the first great Inca ruler

Sam and Liz,
Hola – there have been some interesting developments! I have a hunch that Pachacuti, the first great Inca ruler, is somehow linked to your piece of weaving. As you know, he built the town at Ollantaytambo and many other places in the region you are heading for. Old Spanish documents are becoming increasingly important in our attempts to piece together what we can of Inca history, and I am going to spend a little more time in the Cuzco archives. I will explain more when I catch up with you tomorrow.
PS Ollantaytambo makes the best chicha in all of Peru – don't you agree?

MACHU PICCHU

Day 18

There was one important place that I particularly wanted to see. The most famous Inca city of them all: Machu Picchu. I can't describe the thrill of entering the city for the first time. It is surrounded by mountain peaks and jungle on every side, and the buildings are in the most extraordinary condition. Very little has changed since the time of the Incas; all that's missing are the thatched roofs. There's no road to Machu Picchu, so we caught the train. Beyond Ollantaytambo the landscape began to change rapidly, and within an hour we were in a completely different environment, a hot, sticky jungle with orchids and butterflies.

The first person to reveal the existence of Machu Picchu to the world outside of Peru was the American explorer Hiram Bingham. When he arrived here in 1911 most of the ruins were still covered in thick forest. Bingham thought he had found the original capital city of the Incas, before Cuzco, and the place that Manco fled to after the invasion of the Spaniards.

From Machu Picchu you can see snowy mountain peaks on every side. The Incas believed mountains were sacred places inhabited by powerful spirits.

The discovery of machu Picchu

In 1911, no-one outside of Peru knew of the existence of this incredible place. Hiram Bingham had travelled to this part of Peru looking for Inca ruins. Two days out from Ollantaytambo he met a farmer who was clearing the jungle to plant crops.

Bingham asked the farmer if there were any interesting ruins in the area, and the farmer told him of some Inca buildings on top of the nearby mountain.

The train to Machu Picchu follows the Urubamba river.

Worship of the Sun was practised at Machu Picchu in a building with a curved wall. It is known as the 'Torreon'.

Beneath the sun temple is a natural cave lined with carved stone. There are large niches cut in the rock where archaeologists think mummies may have been housed.

...ne farmer and a small local boy ...uided Bingham 600 m up the jungle- ...overed hillside. There Bingham made ...ne of the best-known discoveries in ...e history of archaeology, machu ...cchu. The city has 200 remarkably ...eserved Inca buildings with the most ...traordinary stonework. The local ...ople always knew about the ruins, ...t archaeologists now call Bingham ...e "scientific discoverer".

Machu Picchu

Camp Machu Picchu

Dr. Orellana arrived at our camp this evening carrying a map of the area. His investigations in Cuzco had proved fruitful, and he had uncovered some exciting information. There was good evidence in the records of the Spaniards that Manco and most of his followers actually settled further west in the Vilcabamba region; not at Machu Picchu as Hiram Bingham believed. In fact, Machu Picchu isn't mentioned anywhere in the Spaniards' records, and it's a mystery what was happening there at the time of the conquest.

Dr. Orellana had seen other documents in the Cuzco archives though, from 1568. These said that the lands of 'Picho' were part of the personal estate of the Inca king Pachacuti; as was another small palace to the north of Machu Picchu, called Guaman Marca. Dr. Orellana pointed to the map. In the unexplored mountains between the two royal estates he drew a circle and wrote the word....Yanacocha!

The Urubamba valley was one of the first regions to be conquered by the great ruler Pachacuti, during the earliest phase of Inca empire-building. After his death his immediate family would have continued looking after his palaces and country estates. The new ruler would have built his own properties.

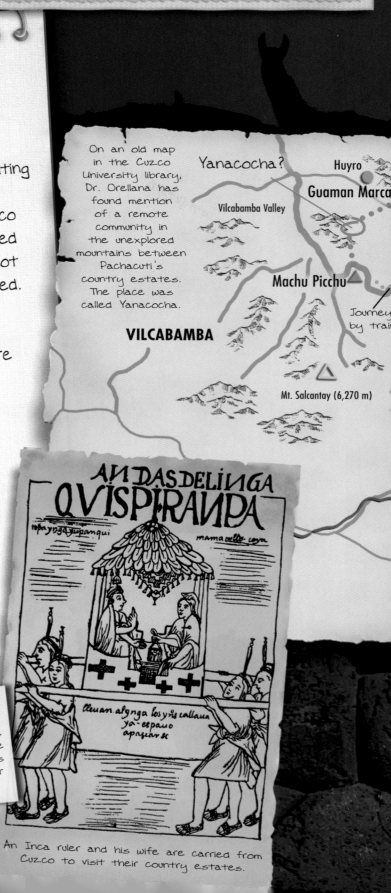

On an old map in the Cuzco University library, Dr. Orellana has found mention of a remote community in the unexplored mountains between Pachacuti's country estates. The place was called Yanacocha.

Yanacocha?

Huyro

Guaman Marca

Vilcabamba Valley

Machu Picchu

Journey by train

VILCABAMBA

Mt. Salcantay (6,270 m)

ANDAS DELINGA QVISPIRANPA

topa ynga yupanqui

mama ocllo coya

cleuan algnga los yris callaua ya-espano apasuar sc

An Inca ruler and his wife are carried from Cuzco to visit their country estates.

Records in the Archbishop's library in Cuzco show that a Father Luis was based in Huyro, a small town near Guaman Marca. Huyro has been the centre for tea production in the valley for many years.

A few years ago, Peruvian archaeologists found signs of an Inca road heading north from Machu Picchu. The jungle was too dense to follow it far, but Dr. Orellana has found out that they are about to try again!

Mt. Veronica
(5,750 m)

Journey by four-wheel drive

llacta

Ollantaytambo

Urubamba Valley

Journey by road from Cuzco

Pisac

▲ Pachacuti site
● Town
▲ Mountain

Sacsahuaman

Cuzco

These llamas are domesticated and have been raised for use as pack animals and for their fibre (wool). They are related to camels.

From: Sir Dennis Barking, The Barking Trust
To: Sam Owen
Subject: Further information from the Barking archives

Dear Sam and Liz,
We have found a letter in the family archives dated September 25th, 1887. It is from a Mr. Edward Mallender, 'The Plantation', Huyro, Peru. Mr. Mallender says in the letter that he felt Sir Cedric would want to hear the news that earlier in the month Father Luis had died. Does this help in any way with your search?

From: Sam Owen
To: Sir Dennis Barking, The Barking Trust

It certainly does! Earlier today, Dr. Orellana located a place called Yanacocha. It is in the hills between Machu Picchu and an Inca site called Guaman Marca. And guess what – there is a town called Huyro nearby! A team of local archaeologists are about to embark on an expedition to follow an unexplored Inca road from Machu Picchu towards Guaman Marca. We are going up to Guaman Marca and will lead a second expedition in the other direction. We will hope to find Yanacocha on the way!

A ROYAL VILLAGE

Day 19

After a bumpy ride in an old four-wheel drive vehicle, we arrived in the village of Guaman Marca. While Senor Rosas, our mule handler and guide, made preparations for the expedition we had a look around the village and the remains of 'Pachacuti's palace'. Compared to Machu Picchu, Guaman Marca is small, simple and rather tumbledown. The palace was built on an artificially levelled piece of land, and was originally made up of four ranges of buildings around an inner courtyard or patio, a bit like a Roman villa. The central courtyard has been used as the village football pitch for many years!

Like Machu Picchu, the site is in a striking position above the Lucomayo river, with good views up and down the valley. Pachacuti and his advisers certainly chose some wonderful natural settings for their architecture.

We set up our tents, and Senor Rosas told us to get an early night. We will be leaving at first light, and could be on the trail for two days.

The ruins of a palace doorway. The stonework of cut granite blocks is very high quality and typical of the architecture of Pachacuti. The site now has a official guardian, a local man, who encourages the children to help look after the ruins and keep them free of vegetation. After all, not every village possesses an Inca palace!

'mas de treinta anos que la dicha Guaman Marca nunca fue sembrada ni cultibada de ningunas chacaras de coca ni de maiz mas de que las dichas tierras fueron de Ynga Yupanqui que tenia alli para su recreacion por no entrar dentro del valle'

Luckily for historians 16th century Spaniards loved keeping records. Dr. Orellana translated this document from 1579. It tells of interviews with the people local to this area, and confirms that the lands of Guaman Marca originally belonged to 'Ynga (Inca) Yupanqui (another name for Pachacuti) para su recreacion' (for his recreation). Just as Dr. Orellana had said, Guaman Marca was one of Pachacuti's country estates!

We put our tents up in the central courtyard. There cannot be much surviving archaeological evidence here because the courtyard has been used by the villagers as a football pitch, and has even been cultivated.

Senor Rosas's men make sure the animals are well shod for the journey. In Inca times the only 'beasts of burden' were llamas. The Spanish introduced horses and mules which can carry much bigger loads.

Senor Rosas made us a delicious supper. This is fried yuca (a root vegetable). It grows on the lower slopes of the mountains.

Tents and food are packed, and loads are measured to ensure that the weight is evenly distributed. Stubborn mules will refuse to move if they are uncomfortable.

Some last minute shopping in nearby Huyro. In the market everything is set out on the ground, including herbs and spices and dyes for the local weavers.

My new Peruvian hat and gloves. Dr. McLeish tells me that traditional designs have been adapted for tourists and for export around the world.

Day 21

The weather has been dreadful. Down in the thicker jungle we were sloshing through deep mud, and at times it was almost impossible to get through the dense undergrowth. However, there have been a couple of surprises.

We'd just set off this morning when Dr. McLeish signalled for us to be quiet. Foraging amongst the thick undergrowth was a young Andean bear or 'spectacled bear'. Dr. Orellana explained that just a few years ago they were under threat in this region. Now they are protected by law, and with responsible conservation of their habitat are making a comeback.

Later, as we cleared a section of Inca road to take a photograph, I noticed a small snake staring at me. Senor Rosas leapt forward and cut off its head with his machete! I was pretty shocked, but Dr. Orellana said it was a deadly coral snake. Senor Rosas has put the head in his pocket. He says he will keep it in the loft of his house as a good luck charm. After that I put on my thickest socks, and I am going to keep my trousers tucked into them.

An Inca road running through the jungle. It is very well built and in good condition. Some sections even have steps.

The Incas built roads through the jungle, across deserts and over high mountains, linking all the diverse environments of their empire. Special state messengers called 'chasquis' ran in relays taking important messages from place to place.

The spectacled bear is South America's only bear. It gets its name from the pale patches around its eyes. Spectacled bears are timid and very rarely seen. They eat fruit, leaves and roots, supplemented by the occasional rodent or insect.

The trail has been easier this afternoon as the jungle has gradually thinned out. We climbed on until dusk, when we noticed the distant shapes of houses and began to hear ferocious barking. We have found Yanacocha. Too tired to write any more...

Houses with thatched roofs and walls of mud brick and plaster. They look the same as Inca houses would have looked 600 years ago.

MYSTERIOUS YANACOCHA

Day 22

We were up at first light. There seems to be no real village, just scattered groups of houses that Dr. McLeish says are each occupied by an extended family, perhaps three generations living together. All the family members look after the children and animals, and share the work on the land. It's a hard life up here; the altitude is about 3,600 metres.

We split up into two groups to do some scouting around. The villagers are very traditionally dressed; the men with brightly coloured ponchos and the women with mantles, or carrying cloths, in which they wrap their babies. Many of the women we saw were busy weaving. In Inca times beautiful textiles were more highly regarded than the finest work in gold or silver, something the Spanish invaders found impossible to understand! We have begun to notice something rather curious: the designs on the villagers' clothing are often quite similar to the tocapus on the Barking textile.

The Andes is the native home of the potato. Even today there are still about 200 varieties grown.

Maize will not grow at this altitude. The principal crop and means of livelihood here is potatoes.

People here still keep herds of llamas, just like in Inca times. The llamas are used to transport potatoes and other merchandise. The villagers often go down to the valley to exchange their potatoes for products like maize.

A group of women weaving on staked-out looms, just as their ancestors did. In Inca times weaving was considered the most important of all art forms.

We found a small, well-built Inca building. Perhaps it was a 'tambo' or way-stop for official Inca travellers. It seems further evidence of the importance of this route.

A small, locked-up church. We asked at the house next door, but they said that they didn't know who had the key. A little strange....

THE TEMPLE OF THE SUN

Day 23

We woke to find the team of Peruvian archaeologists had arrived the previous night, from Machu Picchu. They had uncovered the other half of the Inca road and followed it out of the jungle straight to Yanacocha.

As we were led by Dr. Orellana and other responsible Peruvians, the villagers agreed to meet with us. We asked if there were other ruins in the vicinity. After talking amongst themselves for a while, the mayor said that they had something they wanted us to see. We walked for about 20 minutes until we reached a rocky outcrop above a lake. We followed the villagers up to the narrow entrance to a cave that was invisible from below, and peered inside. Within the cave, highlighted by a beam of early morning sun and carefully placed in a carved niche, was a mummy! I asked Dr. Orellana what he thought. Looking rather pale, he said 'I've never seen anything like this before. It's like a small, lonely temple of the sun'.

One of the Peruvian archaeologists talks to the community council. The council is made up of the heads of all the leading village families.

From the mummy's position in the niche, you could see straight towards the snowy peak of Mount Veronica. The sun must rise almost directly behind it.

The mummy was in a flexed position — the hands folded across the body. Most of the original wrappings were gone.

The cave was lined with cut granite blocks, and the natural rock had been carved with steps.

The ground was covered in burnt offerings. Amongst these we found a wooden kero — the twin to the one in the Barking collection!

From: Sam Owen
To: Sir Dennis Barking, The Barking Trust
Subject: The end of the quest?

Dear Sir Dennis,

Resuming where I left off yesterday — you will never guess what happened next! As we left the cave, Dr. Orellana spoke in Quechua to the mayor. He asked whether the mummy had ever been wrapped in anything else. The mayor began to smile and told us to follow him once more. He took us back to the chapel we had seen the day before, pulled out a key he kept hidden in a small woven bag and opened the door. The interior was very plain, but contained a little statue of the Christ child. The mayor bent down and dragged out a wooden box from beneath the statue. He lifted the lid and took out a brightly coloured weaving. It was a man's tunic, with a square section missing! The mayor explained that long ago the tunic had belonged to the mummy, but when the church was built it was brought here. As far as he could remember, it had always been in the box under the altar. His grandparents had told him that when they were young a priest from the valley had cut a piece off and taken it away. Since then, the chapel had always been kept locked.

THE END OF THE STORY

One week later

This morning we met in Dr. Orellana's study to piece together all the different elements from our trip, just like a team of history detectives. Dr. Orellana stressed that his theory was highly speculative, but I still found the story fascinating.

Machu Picchu, the private estate of the great Inca ruler Pachacuti, would have been maintained by Pachacuti's family from his death in 1490 until the Spanish conquest. When Manco fled into the nearby region of Vilcabamba with many of the royal mummies from Cuzco, perhaps members of Pachacuti's family decided to retrieve some of their important mummified ancestors from him. As the invaders moved ever closer to Machu Picchu, maybe Pachacuti's family took one mummy they valued up the Inca road to Yanacocha, a remote place where it might be kept in safety. Machu Picchu itself was abandoned and was quickly engulfed by the jungle.

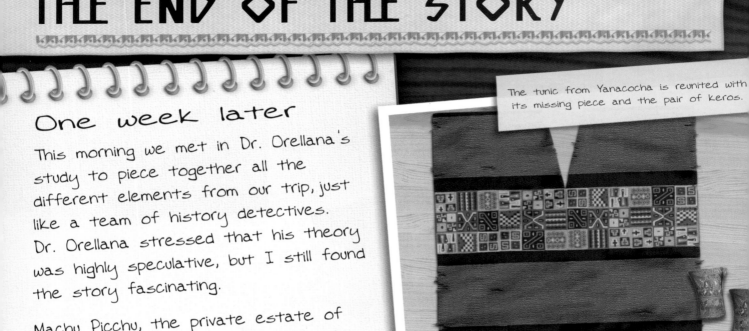

The tunic from Yanacocha is reunited with its missing piece and the pair of keros.

Recent burnt offerings of maize, potatoes and coca leaves were found at the cave. It seems the mummy had become a powerful focus for traditional religious rituals, and had come to be honoured as the ancestor of the whole community. During special ceremonies, the mummy would even have been offered chicha from the keros.

A present for dad. More than just a tourist item, pan-pipes have been played in Peru for more than 2,000 years.

THE STORY OF THE CONQUISTADORS

Manco, his wives, sons and their followers lived in exile for nearly 40 years. In 1572, the Spaniards finally invaded Vilcabamba, and the last of the Inca rulers, Manco's youngest son, Tupac Amaru was executed.

The effects of the conquest were devastating. Millions of people died, while others were forced to leave their homes to work for the invaders in mines or on farms. But high in the mountains small communities lived quietly. For hundreds of years they have maintained their way of life, and their traditions have thrived.

Another strange item in Dr. Orellana's office. The Incas had no writing system, but used these devices of knotted and coloured strings called quipus. The positioning of the knots followed a code which could be used to record important information. Some quipus may have been used as a form of calendar; possibly they were Inca history books. No-one knows for sure.

An extension of their great skill as weavers, the Incas built bridges of braided rope to span Andean rivers. Today only one community in the whole of Peru makes them.

From: Sam Owen
To: Sir Dennis Barking, The Barking Trust
Subject: The story of the Yanacocha mummy

Dear Sir Dennis,

We have now unravelled a lot of the story. Padre Luis performed mass from time to time in the church at Yanacocha, and it must have been him who snipped off the piece of the tunic and somehow obtained the wooden cup. It seems he knew nothing of the cave. Its existence was a closely guarded secret a century ago. But why did the villagers decide to share their secret with us now?

Dr. Orellana says they were exhausted by the dimly remembered duty of protecting the mummy in the cave. They knew that one day looters might destroy or steal everything. When bartering potatoes in Ollantaytambo, they had seen the little museum and decided it was a good time to put their precious objects somewhere like that. They could share the responsibility and the knowledge of these things with others.

A grand opening

Tonight was the official opening of the City Museum's new 'Barking Gallery'. Sir Cedric's collection is now on display alongside material from our recent expedition to Peru. A small delegation had travelled from Yanacocha, and the highlight of the evening was their presentation of a replica tunic to Sir Dennis and Dr. McLeish.

The new gallery is devoted to the people of the Andes, both ancient and modern. It is a fantastic illustration of the main thing that I have learnt from this whole extraordinary adventure: that the study of the past is not only about digging things up, or peering at old documents. In a traditional society, like the one we visited in highland Peru, the way people live now and what they have to tell us can give us an insight into life in ancient times. As long as we listen properly, they can help solve many of the mysteries of the past.

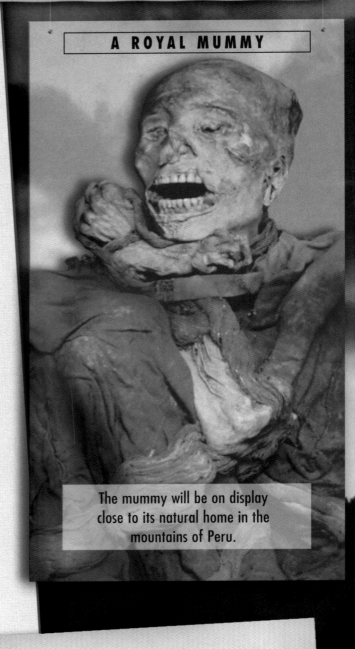

A ROYAL MUMMY

The mummy will be on display close to its natural home in the mountains of Peru.

Dear Liz, Sam and Sir Dennis,

Thank you my friends for leaving the textile fragment in Cuzco, and for sending the kero back. I am sad not to be with you tonight, but I had to stay for an important meeting. It was worth it however, as we have now secured funding to display the mummy and the other artefacts close to their natural home. Hairs and other residues on the tunic match up with the mummy, confirming that they were originally together. We would appear to have something quite unique, an Inca royal mummy. But who was it? Is it a lesser Inca prince, or – as some in the media have suggested – are we looking at the embalmed features of Pachacuti himself. You know that I enjoy a little speculation, but we must be careful not to get too carried away. There is so much more to study. In the future we may find answers to our questions. For now, my best wishes and thanks to you all. We will look forward to seeing you here at the opening of our new gallery. Jorge Orellana

THE REPLICA TUNIC

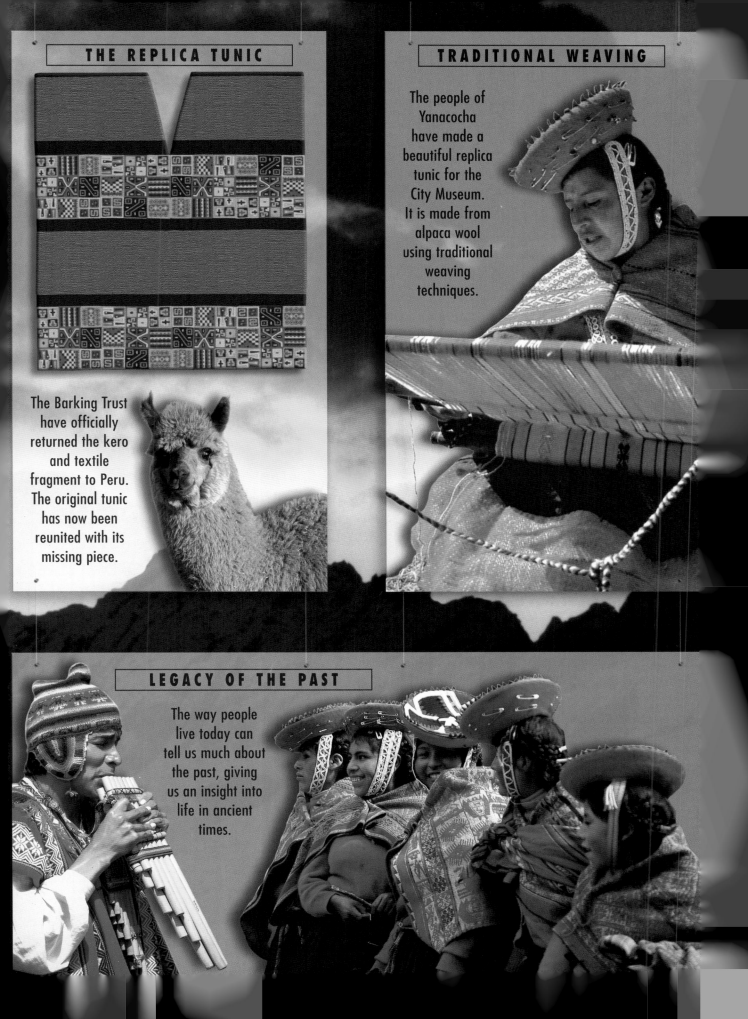

The Barking Trust have officially returned the kero and textile fragment to Peru. The original tunic has now been reunited with its missing piece.

TRADITIONAL WEAVING

The people of Yanacocha have made a beautiful replica tunic for the City Museum. It is made from alpaca wool using traditional weaving techniques.

LEGACY OF THE PAST

The way people live today can tell us much about the past, giving us an insight into life in ancient times.

GLOSSARY

Acclimatize To adapt to a new climate or situation.

Alpacas Domesticated animals found in Peru. They are related to llamas and are raised for their thick fibre (wool).

Altitude The height of a place above sea level.

Ancestors The people in the past from whom you are descended. Normally further back than grandparents.

Archaeologists Scientists who study the past by examining the physical remains left behind.

Archives Collections of historical documents and records.

Artefacts Objects made by humans, for example a tool or pot. Often they are the subject of an archaeological study.

Chasquis Special Inca state messengers. They ran swiftly in relays, taking important messages from place to place.

Chicha Beer made from maize.

Civil war A war between two groups of people from the same country.

Coca leaf tea A tea made from the leaves of the coca bush.

Conquest To take over and possess something, normally territory in a war.

Conquistadors The Spanish conquerors of South America.

Conservation The scientific process of cleaning, mending and preserving ancient objects.

Curator Senior member of the staff of a museum, in charge of its collections.

Delegation A group of people chosen to represent others. Sometimes a delegation represents their country.

Diplomacy Dealing with people carefully and tactfully so as not to upset them.

Embalmed When a body has been treated, normally with some sort of chemical, to stop it from rotting.

Erosion The process by which a rock or a landscape becomes worn away. Weather, rivers, landslides and walking animals all cause erosion.

Estate A large property, usually in the countryside. An estate normally includes a large house, palace or castle and lots of ground.

Fieldwork Studies or research done by students and sometimes by qualified experts (such as museum curators) outside of the classroom or normal place of work. Often in a foreign country.

Granite A very hard type of rock used for building.

Kero A wooden goblet. It would have been used by the Incas for drinking chicha (maize beer) in special rituals or celebrations.

Llamas Domesticated animals found in South America. They are used as pack animals and are also raised for their fibre (wool). They are related to the camel.

Niche A small alcove or recess in a wall.

Quechua The language of the Incas. Millions of people in Peru still speak Quechua today.

Quipus Devices made of coloured and knotted strings. The positioning of the knots followed a code which could be used to record important information.

Ransack To go through a place randomly stealing things and causing chaos and destruction.

Ransom The price demanded or paid for the release of a captured or kidnapped person.

Siege A military operation in which a city or fortified place is surrounded so that no-one can get in or out. The idea is to force the captives to surrender.

Spirit Invisible essence of a personality. Another word for 'soul'.

Stonemasonry The cutting and preparing of stone for use in building.

Temple A building used for worship.

Textile A piece of woven or knitted cloth.

Tocapus Miniature boxed-in designs that were used in Inca weaving.

Trepanation An operation during which a circular hole is cut into a person's skull.

INDEX

t=top, b=bottom, c=centre, l=left, r=right, OFC=outside front cover, OBC=outside back cover

Alamy: 3br, 3bl, 5tc, 7c, 14-15, 14bl, 17tr, 17cr, 21tr, 22-23, 28-29. Adriana von Hagen: 25c, 28tr. Corbis: 6br, 7cr, 7br, 9tr, 10tr, 12-13, 12tr, 13br, 15br, 20-21. David Drew: 8tr, 11cr, 11br, 12br, 15tr, 15cr, 18tr, 18br, 19tl, 19cr, 19cl, 20tr, 21br, 22br, 23cr, 23br, 23bl, 24cr, 24bl. Dumbarton Oaks, Washington, DC: 4br. National Geographic Image Collection, Washington, DC: 14br, 15bl. Natural History Museum: 20bl. Werner Forman Archive (British Museum): 5tl.

Every effort has been made to trace the copyright holders, and we apologize in advance for any unintentional omissions. We would be pleased to insert the appropriate acknowledgements in any subsequent edition of this publication.